Neighborhood Safari

Spiders

by Martha London

FOCUS
READERS®

PIONEER

www.focusreaders.com

Focus Readers is distributed by North Star Editions:
sales@northstareditions.com | 888-417-0195

Produced for Focus Readers by Red Line Editorial.

Photographs ©: Shutterstock Images, cover, 1, 7, 8, 13, 14, 17, 18; iStockphoto, 4, 21 (spider); Nuridsany et Perennou/Science Source, 11; Red Line Editorial, 21 (chart)

Library of Congress Cataloging-in-Publication Data
Names: London, Martha, author.
Title: Spiders / by Martha London.
Description: Lake Elmo, MN : Focus Readers, [2021] | Series: Neighborhood safari | Includes index. | Audience: Grades 2-3
Identifiers: LCCN 2020002184 (print) | LCCN 2020002185 (ebook) | ISBN 9781644933565 (hardcover) | ISBN 9781644934326 (paperback) | ISBN 9781644935842 (pdf) | ISBN 9781644935088 (ebook)
Subjects: LCSH: Spiders--Juvenile literature.
Classification: LCC QL458.4 .L65 2021 (print) | LCC QL458.4 (ebook) | DDC 595.4/4--dc23
LC record available at https://lccn.loc.gov/2020002184
LC ebook record available at https://lccn.loc.gov/2020002185

Printed in the United States of America
Mankato, MN
082020

About the Author

Martha London writes books for young readers. When she's not writing, you can find her hiking in the woods.

Table of Contents

CHAPTER 1

Building Webs 5

CHAPTER 2

Eight Legs 9

THAT'S AMAZING!

Spider Silk 12

CHAPTER 3

Eating Insects 15

CHAPTER 4

A Spider's Life 19

Focus on Spiders • 22

Glossary • 23

To Learn More • 24

Index • 24

Building Webs

A bug flies into a spider's web. The spider crawls toward the bug. It wraps the bug in silk. Then the spider eats the bug.

There are thousands of kinds of spiders. They live in many **habitats** around the world. Some spiders are tiny. Others are big enough to eat birds. Most spiders are not dangerous to people.

Fun Fact

The diving bell spider can live underwater.

Chapter 2

Eight Legs

Spiders have eight legs.

Most spiders have eight eyes.

Some spiders have hairy

bodies. Others are smooth

and shiny.

A spider's body has two sections. The legs attach to the front section. The rear section is called the abdomen. It has the spider's spinnerets. These small body parts release the spider's silk. Spiders use silk to build webs.

silk

spinnerets

abdomen

leg

mouth

Spider Silk

All spiders create silk. But not all spiders spin webs. Spiders can use their silk to build or climb. The silk is stretchy. It does not break easily. Spiders can hang from it. They can also use silk to wrap **prey**.

Chapter 3

Eating Insects

Most spiders eat insects. Many spiders catch insects with sticky webs. Other spiders hunt on the ground. They hide in holes and **surprise** prey.

Many spiders do not chew their food. Instead, they bite prey with their **fangs**. The fangs contain **venom**. The venom turns the insects into liquid. The spiders drink this liquid.

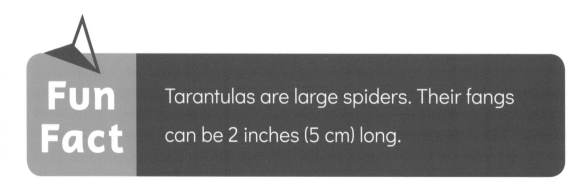

Fun Fact Tarantulas are large spiders. Their fangs can be 2 inches (5 cm) long.

Chapter 4

A Spider's Life

Spiders are **arachnids**. They lay eggs. A female spider makes an egg sac. She covers the eggs in silk to protect them.

Tiny spiders hatch from eggs. They have **exoskeletons**. Young spiders **molt**. They lose their hard skin. A bigger skin grows back.

Most spiders live alone. Each spider eats many insects. Spiders help keep the number of pests low.

Life Cycle

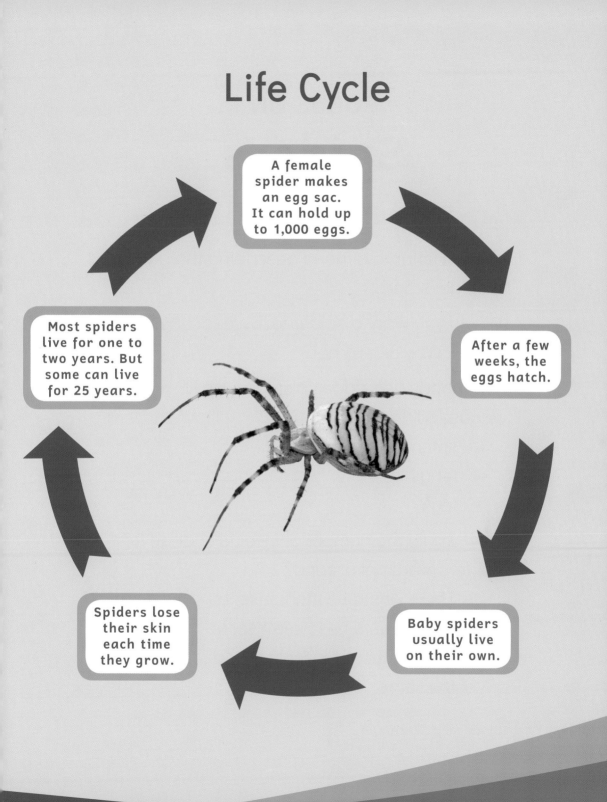

A female spider makes an egg sac. It can hold up to 1,000 eggs.

After a few weeks, the eggs hatch.

Baby spiders usually live on their own.

Spiders lose their skin each time they grow.

Most spiders live for one to two years. But some can live for 25 years.

FOCUS ON
Spiders

Write your answers on a separate piece of paper.

1. Write a letter to a friend describing the parts of a spider's body.

2. Would you want a spider to live near your home? Why or why not?

3. What body parts does a spider use to release silk?
   - A. spinnerets
   - B. fangs
   - C. legs

4. How would the number of insects change if spiders were not around?
   - A. There would be more insects.
   - B. There would be fewer insects.
   - C. The number of insects would stay the same.

Answer key on page 24.

Glossary

arachnids
Animals with exoskeletons and eight legs, such as spiders and scorpions.

exoskeletons
Hard shells that protect animals' bodies.

fangs
Long, sharp teeth.

habitats
Places where an animal lives.

molt
To lose feathers, fur, skin, or shells and grow new ones.

prey
Animals that are eaten by other animals.

surprise
To come without warning.

venom
Poison that comes from an animal's sting or bite.

To Learn More

BOOKS

Higgins, Melissa. *Splendid Spiders*. North Mankato, MN: Capstone Publishing, 2020.

Vilardi, Debbie. *Why Do Spiders Make Webs?* Minneapolis: Abdo Publishing, 2019.

NOTE TO EDUCATORS

Visit **www.focusreaders.com** to find lesson plans, activities, links, and other resources related to this title.

Index

E
eggs, 19–21

F
fangs, 16

L
legs, 9–10

P
prey, 12, 15–16

S
silk, 5, 10, 12, 19

W
webs, 5, 10, 12, 15

Answer Key: **1.** Answers will vary; **2.** Answers will vary; **3.** A; **4.** A